The Mali Empire

A Captivating Guide to One of the Largest Empires in West African History and the Legendary Mansa Musa

Free Bonus from Captivating History
(Available for a Limited time)

Hi History Lovers!

Now you have a chance to join our exclusive history list so you can get your first history ebook for free as well as discounts and a potential to get more history books for free! Simply visit the link below to join.

Captivatinghistory.com/ebook

Also, make sure to follow us on Facebook, Twitter and Youtube by searching for Captivating History.

Contents

Introduction

History, like many other facets of our culture, often revolves around the past of Western countries. In schools and TV programs, in books and blogs, most of the common topics are linked to ancient Rome or Greece, medieval kingdoms, colonial empires, modern conflicts, and scientific revolutions, all of which can be linked with "Western-centric" civilizations. These topics are indeed important, as they reveal parts of our past. Yet, they leave many blank spots in the loom of history. Even worse, these voids aren't merely leaving us without the full story; they also often influence us to see the entire story of humankind from a skewed perspective.

While some of the non-Western peoples managed to fight their way into historiography, for example, Chinese and Arabic civilizations, many others are left out of the historical stage. The sole exemption to this is when they are mentioned as objects of another country's past, like as targets of colonial expansion and conquests. Some of these peoples and nations have managed to garnish some additional attention in recent decades, thanks to both global societal trends and local efforts. However, pre-colonial sub-Saharan Africa remains in a historical vacuum for most people.

The goal of this guide is to break that seal and introduce you to the wealthy and grand Mali Empire, which was just one of many African realms. We will guide you through its inception and follow its rise to prominence. The story then paints Mali's greatness under Mansa Musa, one of the most famous African rulers; he is sometimes regarded as the wealthiest man who ever lived. Then, this guide will turn to the empire's gradual demise. In the process, this book will show that Mali and the rest of the African states weren't isolated cultural lands but part of the global history, influencing each other and faraway nations. Finally, it will try to present some of the unique cultural characteristics of the Malian people in an effort to exhibit the long-existing diversity among the various African nations.

With any luck, by the end of this short but exciting guide, you'll have a fuller picture of our shared past. We hope the book arouses your interest in learning more about the blank spots left in the tapestry of history.

Chapter 1 – West Africa before the Rise of Mali

To understand the story of the Mali Empire and its people, we first have to take a closer look at the broader region in which it was situated, both in terms of history and geography. As with all nations, the roots of Mali are much deeper and wider than they may seem from the surface.

With that in mind, it is important to define the region of West Africa since it has different interpretations. In purely geographical terms, West Africa could encompass a large swath of land from modern-day Morocco up to the South African Republic, covering almost the entire Atlantic coast of the continent. However, when culture and politics are accounted for, the region of West Africa is much smaller. It is bordered by the Atlantic Ocean on its west and south, while the Sahara Desert roughly represents its northern edge. Its eastern rim is usually marked at the Benue Trough, though some extend its border a bit more eastward into what is today Cameroon and Chad. In general, the eastern edge of the region roughly corresponds with the eastern borders of present-day Niger and Nigeria. Even so, the West African region is still quite sizeable, covering roughly two million square miles (five million square kilometers), which equates to about half the size of the entire European continent.

As could be expected in a region that large, there are several different climate and biosphere zones. In its most southern area, on the northern coast of the Gulf of Guinea, lies a tropical zone, which is largely covered with humid broadleaf forests and jungles. Going farther north, one will find the tropical savanna known as the West Sudanian savanna. This zone is dominated by large grasslands and sparse trees, with high temperatures and seasonal rainfalls. As you go northward, the tropical savanna slowly gets drier and hotter, turning into the tropical semi-arid Sahel zone. This biozone also has seasonal rainfalls but in much lesser quantities, making it even less forested than the West Sudanian savanna. Yet, even so, the Sahel still has its fair amount of flora and fauna diversity, especially in terms of migratory animals. Finally, at the northernmost edges of West Africa, the Sahel turns into the Sahara Desert, which is known for its arid climate and low biodiversity. Nevertheless, it's worth pointing out that the Sahara, as the largest hot desert on Earth, has its own subdivisions. As such, on the boundary with the Sahel, the Sahara Desert still has some arid steppe and shrubland regions. These areas have some flora and fauna, no matter how sparse they may be.

Most of West Africa is flat, with the exception of the Guinea Highlands, the Jos Plateau, and the Aïr Mountains, with the latter being the tallest at about 6,600 feet (2,000 meters). Another important geographical characteristic of the region is its rivers, most of which are located in the coastal regions, such as the Senegal, the Gambia, and the Volta Rivers. However, the Niger River, one of the largest in Africa, is somewhat of an exception. Starting from the Guinea Highlands, it flows northeast toward the Sahara before turning southeast around the city of Timbuktu and sprawling into a massive delta in modern-day Nigeria. As such, it represents a major water source in the drier regions of West Africa, and it also acts as an important trading route. The massive river and its trade route were also pivotal for the medieval Mali state, as it formed around the Upper Niger, roughly around the area of Mali's modern-day capital of Bamako. Contributing to the importance of the region between the upper flows of the Niger and Senegal Rivers are plentiful goldfields.

However, before the Malian state came into existence, there was a long history of humans in the region, including some precursor states. As could be expected for a region located in Africa, the cradle of humanity, the first signs of humans in West Africa might even predate the evolution of modern humans or *Homo sapiens*, though archaeologists are still debating over the exact timeline. What seems likely is that the Early Stone Age humanoids arrived in the region to permanent dwell sometime between seventy thousand and thirty thousand years ago. They slowly spread toward the coast. Interestingly, so far, the only archaeological site that indicates a possible earlier settlement is located in Mali, some 160 miles (257 kilometers) south of Timbuktu. At the Ounjougou site, scholars have found some artifacts that date as far back as 190,000 years ago. Furthermore, while the early humans continued to spread across West Africa, this site shows a continuous human presence, as well as one of the earliest appearances of pottery in Africa at around 9400 BCE.

While this site was reaching new heights, the entire continent went through what scientists dub the African humid period. Starting roughly fifteen thousand years ago, the West African monsoon brought much higher levels of moisture, turning the Sahara into a large grassland covered with various rivers and lakes. With that change, some of the West African humans migrated north. In some cases, these Saharan people developed pastoralism, while the groups in the south mostly remained hunter-gatherers. Yet, this wet period didn't last for long, as after several thousands of years, the climate once again began to dry up. Somewhere around 5,500 years ago, the Sahara was once again becoming a desert region, and many people living there began migrating back south.

As the aridness spread, it seems that agriculture began appearing in the central Sahara. Some scholars argue it was transferred to the region from North Africa, possibly Egypt, while others think that it developed independently. In any case, agriculture most likely appeared as a means to supplement the shrinking subsistence sources. It was practiced on a seasonal basis, with the people still relying on pastoralism, hunting, and gathering. Thus, agriculture began to spread with human migrations from the central Sahara to the rest of West Africa, allowing the development of more complex societies.

One of the earliest distinct cultures was formed around 2000 BCE in what is today southeastern Mauritania. It was named the Tichitt culture after the region in which it was found. As of today, it is the oldest civilization linked with the Mandé people, one of the major ethnolinguistic groups of West Africa. Its later descendants would build large empires in the region, including Mali. Over the centuries, the Tichitt civilization developed early forms of urbanism, including fortified towns, various types of art and pottery, and early metallurgy. By the early 1ˢᵗ millennium BCE, they had adopted ironworking. All of this indicates a rather developed social structure. However, the continued aridification of the region began to weaken those societies, and many of the Mandé people migrated eastward toward the Upper and Middle Niger River.

Influenced by these migrations, new urban centers rose in what is today central Mali, mostly in the Mopti and Ségou regions. The most notable settlements are the modern-day archaeological sites of Méma, Macina, Dia (Jà), and Djenné-Djenno. Some of them, especially the latter, show clear signs of influence from the Tichitt culture, which also links them with the Mandé peoples. However, it is worth pointing out that the human settlement of these regions predates these migrations. Yet, as the Mandé moved into the region in the early 1ˢᵗ millennium BCE, these societies began to rise and form city-states. The latest to make that transition was Djenné-Djenno, which scholars usually date to around 250 BCE. Over time, they developed their own interconnectedness. They traded with each other and further developed technologies. While we dot these archaeological locations as single societies, it is vital to note that some of these sites aren't always linked to a single town. Rather, they sometimes cover wider areas, overseeing various urban centers that rose and were then abandoned over the course of several centuries.

Another important notion to remember when reconstructing West African history is that civilizations and societies developed in other locations as well. A few examples are the Nok culture on the Jos Plateau, located in the center of present-day Nigeria; the town of Gao on the eastern side of the Niger River bend; and ancient Ghana, which was centered in modern-day southeastern Mauritania and western Mali. Of course, people also lived along the Atlantic coast, with varying degrees of development. Yet all of these societies had some level of trading connections, with only a few remaining relatively isolated. An illustration of that would be the societies that formed in what is today Sierra Leone, as they were cut off from other West African nations by the dense tropical rainforests. Even more importantly, West Africa as a region was also connected to the Mediterranean and North Africa. Though historians can't point out the exact start of trans-Saharan trade, it is clear it existed in some form prior to the 1st millennium BCE.

There were several caravan trade routes, but the most important ones usually went north or northeast from the region of Timbuktu or Gao. These routes would trail through the Sahara before reaching the Mediterranean coast. Thus, West African gold and ivory reached ancient Egypt, Carthage, and Rome, and in return, it received cloth, beads, salt, and various metal tools. Unfortunately, this trade route also transported slaves, which is evidenced by various Roman and Greek sources. However, this doesn't mean that African or Mediterranean traders met each other or dealt directly. Trade was mostly conducted through middlemen, most notably the various Berber tribes of North Africa.

The existence of these connections was also used in older historiographies to explain the various technological advances of the West African cultures, most notably in the realm of metallurgy. It was hypothesized that trade disseminated knowledge from the Mediterranean world across the Sahara. However, many modern scholars tend to disagree with those theories because some archaeological evidence points to a degree of indigenous technological advances made in the West African region.

Approximate trade routes of the trans-Saharan trade

In the early centuries of the 1ˢᵗ millennium CE, the trade across the Sahara began to intensify as the Berber middlemen began using domesticated camels to help them cross the vast and hostile desert. Yet, the true expansion of trans-Saharan trade came in the 7ᵗʰ century CE when the Arabs took over the Mediterranean coast of Africa. The enormous Umayyad Caliphate, which stretched from the Indus River to the Iberian Peninsula, was in need of gold to sustain its economy and monetary system. However, there weren't any gold mines in North Africa; thus, the local authorities had to acquire it from afar, with one of the sources being West Africa. While it seems that the region wasn't a primary gold supplier to the North African Arabs, trading ties were firmly established. This proved to be crucial for the development of the Sahelian realms, as their newly found prosperity allowed for the creation of the first major states in the region. Both Ghana and Gao expanded and transformed into what historians today classify as empires or kingdoms.

Unfortunately, the exact details of these changes remain largely a mystery. While West African societies developed and adopted various technologies, they didn't leave behind written records from this period. The reason behind this is somewhat disputed. Some scholars claim that most of the states in the Sahel still hadn't invented writing. Others claim that there are signs of written scripts but that these were only used to keep trading records, not for writing historical accounts. It is also possible that their records were created on less durable materials, which simply didn't survive. While there is no conclusive answer to this debate yet, it is more than plausible that various states had some form of markings but hadn't fully transitioned into using a written language as we understand it today. Regardless of the reason, the fact is that the only written historical sources available to modern scholars were made by various Arab travelers and traders in the later centuries. Among other details, they noted some of the oral traditions of the West African nations they encountered.

Trading with the Arabs also brought cultural changes. The most notable and probably the most impactful was the gradual adoption of Islam. Over the following centuries, this religious system slowly and peacefully penetrated the West African region. This was mostly caused by trade, as it made dealing with the Arabs and the now Islamized Berbers easier and more fruitful. The adoption of Islam was also eased by the appeal of its religious tenets, as well as the fact that it didn't fully contradict the traditional West African beliefs. Another important point is that Islam also went through minor local modifications and aligned with preexisting traditions. Thus, it wasn't forced upon by the people but gradually accepted. Despite that, not all rulers accepted the new religion, like, for example, in the Ghana Empire. Nevertheless, they tolerated and accepted the spread of Islam across their lands. In contrast, Gao's sovereigns fully accepted and helped the propagation of Islam, converting themselves in the late 10th century. The spread of the new religion was also helped by various local and foreign scholars and clerics.

With Islam came the proliferation of Arabic influences on other aspects of life, most notably the spread of literacy in the form of the Arabic script. Along with that came transfers of various other technologies, knowledge, and customs. For example, many of their administrative and judicial practices were taken from the Arabic world. Architectural influences and techniques were also pronounced, most notably in the mosques and other buildings related to Islam and its worship. Other cultural changes were observable in familial structures and the position of women in society. While these helped West African societies evolve and transform, Islam also brought an idea that was broader than tribal, ethnic, or linguistic ties. This was a double-edged sword for the West African nations. It allowed for the bonding and formation of larger states and societies, but it also established a separation between Muslims and non-Muslims, creating fertile soil for conflicts.

Thus, by the late 10th and early 11th centuries, West Africa was a sprawling region with many different states, societies, and cultures rising and expanding across its vast lands. They developed their own indigenous civilizational traits but also received influences from afar, forming numerous unique local cultures and traditions. This was possible due to both internal connections and trading but also because of their long and prosperous ties with the Mediterranean world.

Chapter 2 – The Emergence of an Empire

When the Ghana Empire ruled large portions of western West Africa, with its influence stretching far beyond its borders, the Manding region, located in what is now southern Mali and northeastern Guinea, seemed to be just another unimportant province. Yet, historical circumstances made it the unexpected birthplace of one of the greatest African empires that ever existed: the Mali Empire.

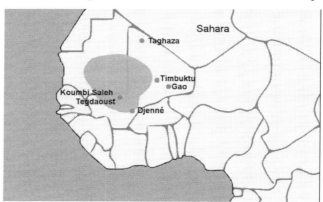

Approximate borders of the Ghana Empire.
(Credit: Barada-nikto, CC BY-SA 4.0 <https://creativecommons.org/licenses/by-sa/4.0>, via Wikimedia Commons; https://commons.wikimedia.org/wiki/ File:Ghana_empire_map-fr.png)

The early history of the Manding region and, with it, the roots of Mali are still somewhat shrouded. However, a rough sketch can be made by combining Arab sources, which were written later; oral traditions of the region that have been recorded more recently; and archaeological findings. The Arab writers report that by the early 11th century, the region had already developed small chiefdoms. They give us the name of two of them: Malal and Daw (or Do). According to these sources, these states were already part of the West African trading network, which explains the presence of Muslim merchants. While the Arab chronicles describe these chiefdoms as kingdoms, they were more akin to city-states. Furthermore, the Arabs describe their towns more like large villages that weren't even walled for protection. Nevertheless, these medieval histories also chronicle that the ruler of Malal converted to Islam in the first half of the 11th century after he witnessed a miracle. While the royal family and some of the nobles became Muslims, the majority of their followers continued to practice their traditional religion.

The oral traditions offer additional details, though there are some variations and regional differences between them. According to one of the traditions, the Manding region was founded by hunters who left the Ghana Empire because of drought or some other misfortune. These hunters formed a brotherhood, which became the root of the mythical twelve tribes and later chiefdoms that constituted the Manding lands. However, there are also other traditions, most notably the ones written down in the Sundiata (alternatively Sunjata) epic. The central myth of the poem is centered around the first Malian emperor Sundiata Keita and the unification of Mali. In its opening passages, it claims that the Manding people came from the east. At first glance, these two traditions may seem irreconcilable, as Ghana is northwest of Manding. Yet, there are some additional details to consider.

Firstly, many of the West African peoples have the notion of coming from the east in their myths. This may have ties with the migrations from the Sahara, or they are possibly later attempts to link themselves directly to their eastern Islamic roots. The Mandé people also had similar traditions. This is important because the Ghana Empire was founded by one of the sub-groups of the Mandé, the Soninké people. On the other hand, the various tribes of the Manding region were settled by the Malinke (also known as Mandinka) and the Bambara people, who are also part of the Mandé ethnolinguistic group. This could explain and reconcile the two myths. On the one hand, the tradition of originating in the east could be a fully fictitious notion or possibly tied with some overarching Mandé memory of their descent from the Sahara. On the other hand, belonging to the same ethnolinguistic group as the Soninké of Ghana could hint at a grain of truth in their ties with the Ghana Empire, though it does not necessarily confirm if the founders were Ghanian or Soninké.

These connections with Ghana are further exemplified by modern tradition that says the Mandé region was part of the empire. It was supposedly known as Ka-Ba (present-day Kangaba), named after one of the Mandé city-states, and it served as the region's capital. However, there is no concrete evidence to back this, even at the height of Ghana's power and extent. It may be that this myth merely depicts close ties, which were probably fueled by trading and ethnic and cultural similarities. Archaeology does confirm some of these traditions. Most notably, the excavated remains indicate that some settlements predate imperial Mali by centuries, some as far back as the 6th century. However, at those early stages, these settlements were far from urban centers, but they grew and increased in complexity over time. Thus, the existence of chiefdoms as developed states and societies is quite likely. Scholars also found evidence of Islamic presence at some of the sites, supporting the idea of Muslim conversion of some Manding residents at a relatively early period, though it is not defined precisely when this conversion began.

With some basic confirmation from the archaeological evidence and through combining the oral traditions and Arab writings, it is possible to give some basic reconstructions of these chiefdoms. They most likely resembled later *kafu,* an organization of several villages under the rule of a single royal or noble clan. These hereditary chiefs later carried the title of *fama;* the early rulers may have held this title as well. These communities were likely small, no larger than ten thousand to fifteen thousand people. The ruling class was the hunters, and it was traditionally hailed as a "supernatural" caste, as these men were thought to have the ability to communicate with nature spirits. In reality, they were vital because they furnished their tribes with food when agricultural products ran low. They also served as an armed force, and they were armed principally with bows and arrows. Apart from the hunters and farmers, it is certain that the Manding chiefdoms also had traders. At some point, gold mining or panning developed, and it seems other forms of mining and metallurgy were practiced as well.

In any case, in the early 11th century, these early Mandé chiefdoms were far from being able to contest Ghana's supremacy. However, the geopolitical situation dramatically changed in the second half of the century. The Ghana Empire began its downward spiral due to internal strife, but its fate was mostly sealed in 1076. According to Arab sources and oral traditions, that is the year the Berber Muslim Almoravid dynasty, which was centered in Morocco, conquered Ghana's capital. Modern scholars debate the historicity of these claims, as there are no contemporary sources or archaeological evidence to support them. However, it is possible the Almoravids merely raided parts of Ghana's territory or politically meddled in its internal conflict, slowly destroying the empire. In any case, by the late 11th and the early 12th century, Ghana's hegemony was ending. Some of the provinces broke off, while the core of the Ghana Empire seems to have been involved in a civil war between the rising Muslim population and the followers of traditional religions.

The early 12th century saw a power vacuum in the region, with new states fighting for supremacy. The sources mention the Soso (or Susu) people, who were among the earliest groups to liberate themselves from Ghanian rule. According to tradition, they are regarded as descendants of the Soninké, and they are most certainly part of the Mandé people. Some modern scholars tend to think of them as one of the Malinke people that got separated because of their refusal to accept Islam. In any case, their center was in the region of Kulikoro, about fifty miles (eighty kilometers) north of present-day Bamako. By around 1180, the Soso had managed to forge their own kingdom or empire, prevailing as a dominant power in the region and conquering many provinces of the former Ghana Empire. According to tradition, around 1200, the greatest Soso ruler, Soumaoro (Sumanguru) Kanté, came to the throne. Under his reign, the Soso Empire grew to its greatest extent. It conquered large portions of the former Ghanian state, including its capital of Koumbi Saleh. After these expansions, Soumaoro turned his gaze upon the Manding region, conquering its Malinke chiefdoms.

The oral tradition of the Malinke, most notably the *Epic of Sundiata*, remembers Soumaoro's reign as being notably harsh toward the Manding population. He was remembered as a despot who terrorized the conquered regions and was an avid opponent of Islam. This prompted the Malinke to rebel against his rule. They followed their hero Sundiata Keita in an uprising.

Here, it is vital to give an explanation of what exactly the *Epic of Sundiata* is, as it represents the primary source of the events that surround the liberation and unification of Mali. It is an epic poem that was passed on through generations of tribal storytellers and musicians called griots. The most common version used in historical research is the one recorded by Djibril Tamsir Niane, a Guinean historian. It was published in the 1960s. Regardless, it is important to remember that there are local variations to the story, and they all, for the most part, contain some legendary elements. Nonetheless, the existence of Sundiata is confirmed by Arab historians who wrote in the 14th century, making it almost certain he existed. Furthermore, while the poem, like any other folktale, has its fair share of exaggerations, it does provide a basic core narrative that is most likely close to the truth. Because of that, it is invaluable in any research of the early history of Mali.

The mythical ancestor of the Keita dynasty, Bilāl ibn Rabāḥ
(16ʰ-century Ottoman miniature).
(https://commons.wikimedia.org/wiki/File:Bilal_(cropped).jpg)

With that in mind, like many medieval literary works, the *Epic of Sundiata* begins by tracing the hero's lineage. It is claimed that the Keita clan was descendants of Bilāl ibn Rabāḥ (Bilali Bunama), a prominent companion of Prophet Muhammad and the first muezzin (the person who proclaims the call to daily prayer) in Islamic tradition. While this is almost certainly a fictitious detail, it creates a strong connection between the Keita clan and Islam. Additionally, as Bilāl was often depicted as being of African descent, it creates a connection between black Africans and the Muslim faith. From then on, the

Malinke poem goes on to explain how one of Bilāl's sons moved to Mali. Then, after several generations, a Keita ruler, Lahilatoul Kalabi, became the first black prince to go on a pilgrimage to Mecca. He was saved by the grace of Allah on his voyage home. With this, the Keita tradition is cemented as being favored by Allah.

The *Epic of Sundiata* continues to describe the two sons of Lahilatoul. The older chose to rule and wield power, while the younger was attracted to fortune, becoming the ancestor of the merchants. This intertwines the Keita dynasty with the trading class while retaining its royal lineage. Lahilatoul's grandson, who was born to the elder son, was Mamadi Kani, who is depicted with the title of *simbon* ("master hunter"). He was supposedly able to communicate with the jinn of the forests and the bush. This ties the Keita clan with the pre-Muslim traditions without conflicting with the Islamic teachings. More importantly, Kani is depicted as a great warrior who managed to conquer the surrounding chiefdoms and clans. His reign is traditionally dated to the mid- to late 11th century, even though there is no clear evidence to prove his existence. Yet, this narrative provides a possible explanation of how the Manding tribes began to consolidate, especially since other evidence points to the unification of chiefdoms under Keita rule in the 11th and 12th centuries.

Other traditions mention that the kingdom of Malal (or Kiri, Daw, or Do) brought about that unity, and the name of that state is further corroborated by Arab sources. Thus, it seems likely that the Keita state could be connected with that name. However, it is important to note that other oral traditions and Arab historians mention that the first king to take the pilgrimage to Mecca was Malal Ling Beremundana (alternatively Beremun or Seremundana). While these sources also connect Islam with the Manding region before the fall of the Ghana Empire, it is hard to make a direct connection with the story of Lahilatoul Kalabi. Thus, while the *Epic of Sundiata* provides an enticing story, it is vital to remember that it is merely one of several oral traditions. Regardless, it seems clear that the Keita dynasty was dominating the Manding region by the early 12ᵗʰ century.

The epic poem lists several more rulers of the Keita dynasty before coming to Naré Maghann Konaté (also called Maghan Kon Fatta). He is depicted as a handsome and beloved king. His reign is dated to the early 13ᵗʰ century, just as the Soso Empire was reaching its peak. He had several wives, which indicates that polygamy was a common practice among the Malinke, at least among the nobles. One of them, Sogolon, was a hunchback and reportedly ugly. However, she was quite strong and bore him a son named Mari Djata. Though the name translates to "Lion King," the child was weak and fragile, and he is often depicted as stiff-legged.

Despite that and the fact he was a younger child, Naré Maghann wanted Mari Djata to succeed him. It was because of a prophecy the old king had received before the birth of his younger son. But Naré Maghann's wish did not come true. Around 1220, his eldest son, Dankaran Touman, took the throne. The epic depicts this as a result of treachery and jealousy, especially from Dankaran's mother, who took the position of primary regent, as Dankaran was only a teenager. However, if there is any truth to this part of the tale, it tells us that it was common practice for the eldest son to succeed.

Regardless, the tale follows the fortunes of Mari Djata and his mother, who were ridiculed even while the old king was alive. Over time, he even became known as Sundiata (or Sunjata). It was an abbreviation of Sogolon Djata ("Sogolon's Lion"), indicating his closeness to his mother. Their torture only worsened under Dankaran Touman's reign (mainly because of Dankaran's mother), and they fled. The traditions and versions of the *Epic of Sundiata* vary on where exactly they went, but they tell us that most other Manding chiefs refused to welcome them for fear of retribution.

Thus, Mari Djata found himself at the court of the king of Méma, a region located north of Massina (or Macina) and west of Lake Debo. The epic conveys this exile happened because Mari Djata miraculously managed to overcome his invalidity and become respected among his peers, making him even more of a threat to his half-brother. Stripping the story of its exaggeration and legendary aspects, it outlines a brewing confrontation for the inheritance, which was won by the elder Dankaran Touman. Despite his victory, Dankaran's fortune was short-lived. Around 1230, Soumaoro Kanté of the Soso came and subdued the Manding region.

Soumaoro's reign is described as tyrannical and oppressive, with the king mercilessly killing men and abducting women. To emphasize his despotic rule, the story conveys that the king even stole his nephew's wife. This was his best general and trusted ally, and the general decided to leave him over this infraction. It was a sign of weakness, which endowed Dankaran Touman with the confidence to try and rebel, but the Soso crushed his uprising quickly. In turn, Soumaoro tried to take direct control over the Manding region while enacting bloody punishments on those who sided with the rebels. While the former Keita king fled, the local Malinke population tried to organize a new uprising, summoning Sundiata to lead them.

Upon reaching his homeland, Sundiata met with the various rebelling clan leaders to gain their pledge of allegiance. Thus, joint forces of several Manding tribes challenged the Soso army on the open battlefield. The initial clashes proved indecisive, but the Malinke were growing in confidence since they had proved to be worthy opponents of what was supposed to be an undefeatable force. The struggle culminated at the Battle of Kirina around 1235, which ended with a conclusive victory for Sundiata and the Manding armies.

The *Epic of Sundiata* does provide some military details of the battle, including the use of cavalry and archers, but there is no sure way to confirm this. Similarly, modern scholars can't really be sure where the battle took place, as some believe that the modern-day town of that name may have been founded later. In any case, the course of the battle has been depicted as hinging more around a magical clash between the two kings, both of whom were described as powerful magicians. In the end, Soumaoro was defeated because Sundiata poisoned him with a bird's feather that had been dipped in poison since the Soso king was impervious to metal.

While these are, of course, fictitious details made to separate two protagonists from being mere mortals, they could also indicate that religion and belief played an important role in the uprising. This idea is furthered when one looks at previous depictions of Soumaoro's persecution of Muslims. At the same time, the poem hints at another more realistic root of Sundiata's victory. The general that abandoned Soumaoro joined the Manding army, and he played an important role in the Battle of Kirina. A defection of such sort may have significantly shifted the balance of power in Sundiata's favor.

In any case, it seems that Soumaoro's defeat was complete. According to the *Epic of Sundiata*, the Soso king fled, never to be seen again. The many surrounding chiefdoms hurried to pledge their allegiance to the Manding. Sundiata proceeded north toward the city of Soso. The nobles of the city attempted to defend it, but it was futile. It was quickly seized and razed to the ground. After breaking the main opposition of the Soso, Sundiata split his army into three bodies, which descended onto Soumaoro's remaining allies. According to some traditions, his forces conquered the regions of Jalo in the Fouta Djallon highlands in central Guinea; Kaabu, located roughly in modern northeastern Guinea-Bissau; Bambougou around the Bambouk Mountains and goldfield; and the city of Kita and its surroundings in what is today the Kayes region in western Mali. Apart from that, Sundiata also visited his mother's homeland, the land of Do, which was located south of the Manding region. All of those regions were supposedly incorporated into Sundiata's state, though there is no concrete evidence for that. It is possible that some regions merely paid a tribute or were conquered later. Nevertheless, it was clear that the Keita clan had become the dominant power in West Africa.

After the conquests were finished and Sundiata felt secure enough, he and his armies returned to Manding. They gathered near the ancient town of Ka-Ba in 1236, where they celebrated their great victory and shared their spoils of war. During the feast, Sundiata was proclaimed the *fama* of *famas*, which means "chief of chiefs" or "king of kings." He was then officially elevated to the newly created title of *mansa* or emperor (or sultan in the Islamic world). Then, all of the chiefs who had gathered there swore fealty to him by ceremoniously giving Sundiata their land by placing spears in front of him. He would return their spears to them, granting them these lands, which they would rule under his aegis. In other words, they officially recognized his sovereignty. That act transformed the nature of their relationship from what was more akin to a Keita-led alliance of Manding chiefdoms into a single unitary state. It was the birth of the Mali Empire.

Chapter 3 – From Strong Foundations to Turbulent Uncertainty

In the year 1236, Sundiata Keita, the Lion King of Mali, managed to establish a new empire that would become known as Mali. Yet, this was merely the beginning of the story for the Malinke domain and the Keita dynasty, as it was destined to achieve much more.

However, before delving into how Sundiata's seed blossomed, it would be pertinent to first discuss the empire's name. Today, it is almost ubiquitously referred to as the Mali Empire, which later lent its name to the modern state in roughly the same region. However, in reality, there is no clear evidence that the medieval Malinke called their state Mali. The oral traditions used the modern lexicon; thus, they cannot be taken at face value when it comes to such details. The Arab writers do mention Mali, but they may have been wrongly informed or merely took the name of one of the royal cities as the name of the entire region. In some cases, they refer to Mali as people. Modern-day Malinke mostly use the terms Manding or Manden when referring to the heartland of the Mali Empire, while scholars tend to classify Mali, Mandé, Manden, and Manding as different pronunciations of the same word. Thus, it is possible that Sundiata and his followers would have referred to their homeland as Manding or some similar variation.

According to some theories, the word Mali itself seems to be of Fula origin, which is another large ethnolinguistic group of West Africa. It was the name that became the most prominent among foreign visitors. Other theories suggest that Mali means either "the place where a king lives" or has its roots in the Malinke word for hippopotamus, an animal that was associated with Sundiata and the Keita dynasty. However, these theories aren't as accepted. Most seem to believe that Mali got its name from the people and land that were at its core. In any case, while it seems the terms Mali and Manding may be interchangeable to a degree, in this book, the latter is used to refer to pre-imperial Mali lands, as our story largely centers around that specific region. Yet, in its imperial history, which covers a much wider area, the term Mali will be used to describe the empire.

Moving past the etymology and naming conventions, after Sundiata defeated Soumaoro and the Soso, he formed a new state, one that was vastly different than before. Most of the neighboring chiefs or kings accepted the sovereignty of the Keita dynasty. But there was more. The *Epic of Sundiata* and other traditions tell us that on the very day the ceremonial transfer of power occurred near Ka-Ba, the newly crowned emperor created a constitution of sorts for the Mali Empire. This was Sundiata's proclamation, known as Kouroukan Fouga (Kurukan Fuga) or the "Division of the World." The exact content is debatable, as it is based on oral tradition, but some generalizations can be made. First, Sundiata dealt with social and governmental organizations. He divided the clans into four major groups. At the top were the four Maghan or "Princely Clans." They were responsible for leadership. Then there was the *Djon-Tan-Nor-Woro* or "Carriers of Quivers." This consisted of twelve to sixteen hunter clans that were responsible for defense. After that came *Mori-Kanda-Lolou* or the "Guardians of the Faith." This was comprised of five clans, which were responsible for religion and teaching. Then came *Nyamakala*, the "Wielders," who had the power of life or creativity. This consisted of four to seven clans that were connected with various crafts and occupations. The last social group was the slaves.

After dividing the roles and duties of the clans, Sundiata regulated their mutual relations. All of the Malinke should be in a *tanamannyonya* (blood pact) and a *sanankunya* (a joking relationship). The latter implicates that people should treat each other as family members, with whom familiar jokes or humorous insults could be exchanged. Sundiata also encouraged his subjects to be honorable to each other, avoid betrayal, and maintain mutual respect. The proclamation also specified that the general succession was patrilinear in accordance with primogeniture and that the Keita clan was the exclusive imperial clan. These rules created a robust structure for the development of the empire and its basic social structure.

However, Sundiata also touched upon other aspects of life. Several articles are linked with marriage. These proclaim the marrying age and dowry, and they also regulate divorce. The emperor stipulated that men shouldn't chase after married women and never offend any women since they were all mothers. One of the rules also says that a married woman shouldn't be beaten before her husband could deal with the issue. Thus, while there were some protective regulations for women, it is clear that they were treated more as objects of the law instead of being addressed directly.

Other aspects of life were also regulated, like ownership, the exchange of goods, and taxes. Yet these seem to have been less detailed and had fewer rules. Sundiata mandated that foreign envoys would be protected and that outsiders shouldn't be mistreated. Education and raising children fell upon the entire society, as everyone shared paternal authority.

There are some rules that are less common in the rest of the world. For example, the emperor told his subjects to be humble and help those in need and that satisfying one's hunger without taking anything more was not stealing. Sundiata also ordered not to burn trees with flowers and fruits, protecting nature from excessive destruction. These rules could be tied with the harshness of the land and climate in Mali. However, the mansa also ordered that slaves shouldn't be mistreated. Similarly, while Sundiata permitted the killing of enemies of the empire, he forbade their humiliation. Finally, he said that all should abide by the laws and that everyone should enforce them. This, in theory, meant that the rules were equal for all, including the nobles and the Keitas. All in all, if tradition is to be believed, this Malian constitution seems quite advanced for its time, at least in some aspects.

Another important factor of the great gathering at Ka-Ba was that it was the foundation of the Gbara or "Great Assembly." It was a deliberative gathering of all the clan leaders and representatives, who met with the emperor to discuss various stately matters. Thus, the mansa's rule never became absolute, unlike other empires. According to the *Epic of Sundiata*, the assembly gathered at the capital, not in the same field near Ka-Ba, and these meetings were less grand and pompous. However, modern scholars disagree on where the capital of Mali was. According to some traditions, including some versions of the *Epic of Sundiata*, the capital was Niani, which was located on the banks of the Sankarani River, near the border between Mali and Guinea. This is corroborated by one Arab source that states "Nyeni" was the Malian capital. Archaeologists have found the site, and it shows signs of having a high-density population at a certain point.

The location itself has some merits for a capital. It is near the Bure goldfields, which were located on the edge of a forest rich with kola nuts and palm oil. Furthermore, Niani had some natural defenses since it was surrounded by a semi-circle of hills and a river, and it was somewhat deeper into the mountains, making it less accessible to large armies. The Sankarani was traversable and linked with the Niger, making it accessible for traders.

While that was enough for many scholars, especially in the previous century, to accept Niani as the Malian capital, some recent researchers disagree. They point to the lack of archaeological evidence, as Arab visitors described significant trade activity. Additionally, many of the unearthed samples have been dated to much later, roughly the 15th century, which makes one wonder if the site was even active during Sundiata's time. Another complicating factor is that most Arab travelers refer to the capital as Mali, while other traditions link it with Ka-Ba itself or Dakajalan (Dakadiala), which was the center of the previous Keita rulers. Manikoro (Mali-Kura) is a possible contender as well.

With so many uncertainties, some historians have proposed that Mali never had a singular capital but that the center of the state was where the emperor found himself as he traversed across his domain. Impermanent capitals aren't unheard-of in Africa, like, for example, in Ethiopia. It also occurred in other parts of the world, including medieval Europe. If that was the case, then it would be possible that all of the traditions and Arab writings are partially true. With that in mind, it is also possible that after the assembly at Ka-Ba, Sundiata moved to Niani for a while to rebuild it as an important economic center. However, this theory has a problem in reconciling the grandeur and importance of the capital reported by the Arab visitors, which seems unlikely if it was an impermanent capital. Yet, these depictions are mostly from the second half of the 14th century, by which time Mali would have had more than one great trading town. Later Keita rulers may have built palaces in several of them. Yet, all the traditions remark that the Mali capital was never outside the Manding region.

Regardless of where the capital was, Sundiata's rule has been remembered as peaceful and prosperous. Villages and towns were rebuilt, and new ones were created as well. Trade prospered, harvests were plentiful, and the mansa's reign was just. According to the *Epic of Sundiata*, the only problem he encountered was with Soumaoro's nephew, who was given Soso to administrate. It seems the general became a bit too independent, prompting the emperor to banish him and confiscate Soso's land for the royal dynasty. Additionally, later on, some other tribes and chiefdoms joined Mali of their own volition.

All in all, there aren't many details on his rule after 1236, even though it lasted to about 1255 or 1260. While it is possible that it was uneventful, it is also possible that some events ascribed to the first year or two of his reign took place throughout his reign. For example, some of the conquests may have happened later on but were merged with the earlier ones. Also, some of the constitutional changes may have been cumulative; they might not all have been a part of the great proclamation.

Yet, these are mere conjectures, as is the death of Sundiata. Traditions offer several versions of how the great emperor died. Some better-known stories say that a stray arrow struck him at a ceremony or that he drowned while crossing the Sankarani. It seems that the only commonality is that Sundiata didn't die of natural causes. Unfortunately, his burial place is unknown, but there are numerous temples and shrines where he is still worshiped today. He was succeeded by his eldest son around 1255, who became known as Mansa Uli (or Ouli) in Arabic sources. Tradition remembers his name as Yérélinkon (alternatively Jurunin Kon or Yérélinkong).

He proved to be a worthy successor of the Lion King, as he maintained Mali's prosperity while also expanding its borders in the Senegambian region. According to some sources, his generals even reached the region of the Lower Senegal River, and some of the Malinke were settled in these newly conquered areas to consolidate imperial control. He was also the first Keita who has been attested to have gone to Mecca on the hajj, which grabbed the attention of the Arabs.

A pottery statuette of a Malian horseman, one of the Mali Empire's light forces.

However, his rule was cut short; he died shortly after returning from a trip around 1270. The crown passed to his younger brother Wati, whose reign was short and unmemorable. Mansa Wati was then succeeded by another brother, Khalifa. Wati and Khalifa aren't remembered by oral tradition, only by Arab writers, which prompted some historians to argue that both of them were adopted sons of Sundiata. This speculation could be confirmed by Malinke lore; in some cases, it mentions Yérélinkon as the only son of the founding emperor. Others claim that the omission was merely because traditional tales only remember rulers with progeny. Another theory is that Arab historians added these two rulers to fit their narrative template of a four-generation cycle of dynastic decline. One of the more recent explanations is that Khalifa, meaning "successor" in Arabic, wasn't a real name. Khalifa is described by the Arab sources as a mad devotee of archery who hunted his own men. This brief description and his questionable name have prompted some to theorize Khalifa was a usurper of some sort, most likely from one of the hunter clans that stood against the Great Assembly.

In that scenario, some of the clans may have used the royal family's instability to wrestle control from the Keitas. The dynasty's vulnerability could have come from the fact that Yérélinkon's son, possibly the only direct successor, was underaged at the time. Or Yérélinkon possibly might not have had sons at all, leaving only nephews from his sisters, Sundiata's daughters, to succeed him. At the time, the Keitas weren't deeply rooted as rulers, despite all of the supposed love and respect for the first mansa. In that case, even Wati could have been a non-Keita ruler.

While these details remain questionable, it seems Khalifa's rule was short and ended in violence, as he was deposed and killed within a year of taking the throne. He was succeeded by Bata Mande Bori, or Abu Bakr in Arab sources, the son of one of Sundiata's unnamed daughters. This may have happened due to a counter-coup victory of a Keita loyalist, explaining the bloody transition of power. While historians aren't sure if insanity or usurpation was the cause of Khalifa's fall, most do agree that a new ruler sat on the Lion King's throne by about 1275.

The new mansa ruled for a much longer time, at least ten years, if not more. However, the sources and traditions are once again silent, offering not even the slightest details of his reign. Modern scholars have nonetheless speculated that it most likely wasn't much more prosperous or stable than that of his immediate predecessors. This is because Bata Mande Bori was deposed. The exact date is debatable, but the earliest proposed year is 1285, although many tend to put this event in the 1290s. The exact year is not as important as the fact that the throne was once again usurped, this time by a man called Sakura. This has prompted some scholars to argue that Bata Mande Bori was chosen as a successor by the Gbara because his maternal Keita lineage made him easier to be manipulated by the nobles. His reign depended on their willingness to accept him as their mansa. In that scenario, Sakura might be a noble who played the political game the best, gathering enough power through various intrigues before simply dethroning his puppet and taking the imperial title for himself.

However, Mansa Sakura's background is also questionable. In some oral traditions and Arab sources, he is mentioned as being a slave. Earlier scholars tended to accept that at face value, thinking of him as a freed slave who was possibly freed by Sundiata himself and was employed at the court in some capacity. Yet, modern historians have discovered that the term "slave" was sometimes used metaphorically for members of client clans, meaning Sakura was more likely a noble of some sort. Some have even theorized he may have been a general who served Sundiata or Yérélinkon. However, the only evidence in favor of this was his military capability. Mansa Sakura led campaigns that expanded the Mali Empire, which, according to some sources, spread from the Atlantic coast to the city of Gao on the Middle Niger. While this is most likely an exaggeration, Sakura definitely conquered a significant area. He certainly pushed eastward, but it is possible he expanded toward the west as well. Not only that, but he also stabilized Mali, making it awe-inspiring and attractive to foreign traders once again.

Mali's stability and prosperity were best illustrated by the fact that Sakura went on his own hajj to Mecca, which was enough for him to be considered one of the great mansas. However, this pilgrimage was only recorded by later Arab writers, not in the Malinke tradition. This has prompted modern scholars to theorize about the reason. Some assume that his non-Keita usurper status meant later emperors wanted to erase Sakura's illustrious rule from the record, as it damaged the reputation of the royal dynasty. Another theory is that many of his achievements, especially the hajj, was actually a misattribution of the later Mansa Musa's deeds as a way to create room for criticizing the mighty emperor.

Whether he was a great ruler or merely an imposter, Sakura's reign was cut short. According to all the sources and traditions, he was killed on his journey back from the pilgrimage near Tripoli. Once again, the exact date is uncertain, but it wasn't before 1300 and most likely not after 1307. He was murdered either by bandits or, as some oral traditions claim, by his successor, Mansa Qu.

The new emperor, alternatively known as Kaw or Gao, was from the Keita dynasty, restoring the family's legitimate rule over Mali. However, his exact linage is a matter of dispute. Most sources claim he was Yérélinkon's son, while in others, he is mentioned as a son of one of Sundiata's sisters or daughters. Anyhow, his reign was brief and uneventful. The only thing we know is that he was succeeded by his son, who is referenced as Muhammad; both of these details were only recorded by Arab sources. Once again, the date of this transition of power is unknown, but an approximation can be made. The death of Sakura occurred between 1300 and 1307, while the rise of Mansa Musa happened between 1307 and 1312. That leaves the rules of Qu and Muhammad a brief window in the early years of the 14th century. In any case, most sources either skip their rules or only briefly mention they existed. The only exception is a single Arab source, written in the mid-14th century, which records a conversation between Mansa Musa and the governor of Cairo.

While the Arab governor was trying to learn more about Musa and Mali, he asked his guest how he became king. The mansa reportedly said that his predecessor had wished to reach the limits of the Atlantic Ocean. He first sent an exploratory mission of two hundred ships. However, only one returned, with its captain claiming all the other vessels had been lost to powerful sea currents. That didn't satisfy

Muhammad, who then supposedly built two thousand more ships, with half of them reserved for provisions. He then sailed across the ocean himself, leaving Mansa Musa as his deputy. Since he never returned, Musa became the mansa in his own right, or so he told the governor. Despite having Musa supposedly as a source, many historians are doubtful of this oceanic exploration. Firstly, no other source, tradition, or archaeological evidence backs the claim, which seems unlikely for such a grand endeavor. Even the initial two hundred ships are an exaggeration, not to mention the latter two thousand vessels. Furthermore, the naval capabilities of coastal societies in the Senegambian region were too primitive for such attempts, as attested by 15th-century Portuguese sources claiming that the local population of that region saw sails for the first time upon their arrival.

Despite that, the description of a powerful current, most likely the Canary Current that indeed facilitated transatlantic travel in later centuries, does indicate that it is possible that, at some point, Senegambian sailors ventured that far into the ocean. If so, it leaves a slight possibility that Muhammad's voyage actually occurred. The silence of the Malinke tradition could be explained by the collective judgment over his abandonment of the throne. Leaving his people for the sake of discovery was shameful, and the people likely hoped he would be forgotten. However, once again, all of these theories are so far merely conjecture. The one thing we know for sure is that, in comparison with Mansa Musa, Qu and Muhammad were mere specks in history.

Chapter 4 – The Golden Age of Mansa Musa

After several weak rulers and one successful usurper mansa, the Mali Empire was reaching a turning point in the early 14th century. The uninspiring reigns of Emperors Qu and Muhammad certainly made the future of the Keita dynasty uncertain. Yet, at that moment, probably the greatest Keita who ever ruled stepped up to restore Mali's glory.

Mansa Musa, also known as Kanku Musa in the oral traditions, became the ruler of Mali under dubious circumstances. While Arab sources mention his own admission of accidentally coming to the throne after Muhammad's disappearance on his ocean travels, some historians suspect that Musa likely disposed of his cousin. Musa was born in the side branch of the Keita dynasty; he was most likely a grandson of Sundiata's brother, Mande Bori. While Mande Bori wasn't as heroic and celebrated as Sundiata, he was remembered as a great hunter and an ally of the first mansa. He was also mentioned in the *Epic of Sundiata*. Having a member of the dynastic side branch on the throne indicates there were some irregularities in the succession. However, he may have been the oldest or most accomplished Keita at the time of Muhammad's demise. In any case, by 1312, Musa took the crown of Mali, marking the beginning of its golden age.

Even so, there aren't many details of Musa's reign. It seems that Musa spent his early years on the throne, stabilizing his empire but also expanding it. While scholars aren't sure exactly when, where, and how he led his campaigns, by the time of his pilgrimage to Mecca in 1324/5, it seems certain that the Mali Empire stretched from the Atlantic coast across the Sahel to and beyond the cities of Timbuktu and Gao. Thus, Mali had conquered the Senegambian states and the local states of Jolof (Wolof) and Tarkur. It had the salt mine region around the town of Taghaza in modern-day northern Mali and the copper-rich region around Takedda, located at the archaeological site of Azelik wan Birni in present-day Niger. The Malian domain also reached as far as the city of Kukya, the original center of the Songhai people on the Niger River near the modern Niger-Mali border. The only direction the Mali Empire didn't spread much was southward, as Manding was its southernmost region.

However, scholars aren't sure where Sakura's addition to the empire ends and Musa's begins. For example, the conquest of Gao has been attributed to both of them. One possible solution is that the city rebelled in the period between the two great mansas, which would mean that Musa merely reconquered it. Another example is the Senegambian coast. Some historians question if Sakura reached that far west, yet Musa states his predecessor was lost at sea, implying that Mali had already reached the Atlantic. However, it is possible that Musa expanded control in that region. The only certain expansion of the empire under Musa seems to be to the north, where he was said to have subdued Saharan nomadic tribes, securing trading routes to the Arab world. It is important to note that Mansa Musa's conquests were at least partially achieved by his generals, with Saran Mandian probably being the most successful since his name was recorded.

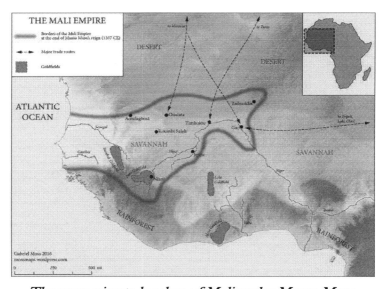

The approximate borders of Mali under Mansa Musa.
(Credit: Gabriel Moss, CC BY-SA 4.0 <https://creativecommons.org/licenses/by-sa/4.0>, via Wikimedia Commons; https://commons.wikimedia.org/wiki/File:The_Mali_Empire.jpg)

In any case, Musa managed to stabilize the Mali Empire and ensure enough support for his rule to be able to leave his country and go on the hajj. If his position as mansa wasn't politically secure, he most likely wouldn't have gone. Additionally, considering the lavish description of his visit left by numerous Arab writers, his voyage required substantial preparations. Musa must have spent at least several years gathering the vast wealth he carried with him. He reportedly took up to 35,600 pounds (16,000 kilograms) of gold alone. To put it in perspective, it would equate to about 930 billion dollars today. This was likely an exaggeration, as well as the size of his retinue. Supposedly, Musa took sixty thousand people with him, with no less than twelve thousand slaves. Nevertheless, it is clear that Mansa Musa was immensely rich, leading to claims of him being the wealthiest man who ever lived. However, this is almost impossible to calculate and compare across historical periods and regions. Nevertheless, it is safe to say that Mansa Musa was quite wealthy.

As to how he managed to gather so much wealth and slaves, there are several sources we can look at. Firstly, there was the already mentioned conquest, which, by Musa's own claims to Cairo's governor, constituted of no less than twenty-four cities, each with its surrounding districts. These would have been the primary source of slaves. Additionally, new lands meant additional tributes and taxes, as well as new trading hubs and resources. Secondly, Takedda proved to be of great importance in the Sahel, as copper was worth two-thirds of the weight of gold because it was relatively rare in the region. Finally, the Mali Empire controlled goldfields, though, by Musa's admission, these weren't in direct control of the royal family. Supposedly, they tried to impose direct control, but it led to the fall of production. Instead, the imperial treasury was filled with tributes and trade with the locals. Other important trading goods were salt and ivory, as well as slaves. All of these were exported to the Arab merchants, adding to Mali's wealth.

After gathering gold and people for his entourage while also securing his throne, Mansa Musa set off across the Sahara to Cairo and then headed on to Mecca. He arrived in Egypt in mid-1324, where he received a warm welcome after the locals, including the governor, witnessed Mali's wealth. On his journey, Musa wanted to show off his riches. Thus, he gave a lot of gold to people, and he also bought a lot of souvenirs and goods to bring back home. For example, he gave no less than 400 pounds (180 kilograms) of gold to the Mamluk ruler of Egypt, while some claim he built mosques and bought homes for future Malian pilgrims. It appears that the amount of gold Musa spent and gave away while in Egypt was so immense that it actually brought down the value of gold in the region. Such bravado was enough for the entire Arab world to take notice of Mansa Musa and the Mali Empire, inspiring the interest of both scholars and merchants.

In that lies the true value of Musa's hajj. Since he brought a number of merchants and nobles with him, he created a new level of diplomatic and mercantile contact between Mali and the Arabs. It is also the reason he became so well known in world history. While Sundiata was remembered largely through oral traditions, Musa was primarily remembered in Arab sources. However, they mostly report details of his pilgrimage, while the rest of his reign is described rather vaguely and in broad strokes. This is how we know that Musa encountered trouble while returning from Mecca to Cairo, as his caravan got separated from their Arab guides. Reportedly, he lost as much as one-third of his retinue to dehydration, hunger, and Bedouin attacks before being rescued. Many other details were also recorded, yet these details are largely inconsequential to the overall history of the Mali Empire.

More important are the reasons behind Musa's pilgrimage. While his own piety certainly played a role, one of the Arab sources portrays it as a redemption journey for accidentally murdering his own mother. While that certainly captures the imagination, it is unclear if there is any truth behind this claim since no other mention of it exists. It could possibly be a reference to court intrigue and that he had to secure his throne by killing his stepbrother's mother or even his grandmother. However, simply trying to atone for such a serious crime wouldn't require such an exhibition of grandeur on his voyage. Instead, it is more likely that Musa's hajj was one of the goals of his pilgrimage. He also wanted to project power to his Malian subjects and quell any question regarding his succession and that of his heirs. This is especially evident since he left his son Maghan (also referred to as Muhammad by Arab sources) as his deputy and royal regent.

A modern artistic interpretation of Mansa Musa,
with Malian cavalry behind him.
(Credit: HistoryNmoor, CC BY-SA 4.0 <https://creativecommons.org/licenses/by-
sa/4.0>, via Wikimedia Commons; https://commons.wikimedia.org/
wiki/File:Empire_mansa_musa.jpeg)

Another reason was to secure new trading connections, gain a larger share and more command over the trans-Saharan trade, and possibly expand Mali's territorial claim. This is evident since at least part of his retinue were merchants. Additional confirmation comes from global history, as Islamic states of northwestern Africa were in decline at the time, making them much less profitable partners. Thus, Malian traders needed to establish new ties with the more stable and prosperous Mamluk Egypt. Finally, Mansa Musa certainly wanted to raise both his personal status and that of his empire on a global scale, which is why he would have spent more gold than was probably imaginable in the medieval Mediterranean.

It seems he managed to attain a number of his goals. There were no recorded upheavals during Musa's reign, and his son did succeed him. During his rule, Mali enjoyed unprecedented prosperity, and it was frequently visited by numerous Arab merchants. However, Musa's final goal was only partially achieved. Mali was recognized as a wealthy land; it was even known in European courts. Yet, his empire never managed to truly become an international power.

Apart from riches and significant global acknowledgment, Mansa Musa's reign proved to be the golden age of the Mali Empire because of cultural advancements. His pilgrimage created greater ties with the Arab sphere. That led to the import of various aspects of Arab culture, from more mundane things like clothing to the more significant things like architecture. Reportedly, Musa even brought a famed Arab architect and poet, Abu Ishaq al-Sahili, back to Mali with him to help in his attempt to uplift the Malian culture. Though modern scholars doubt the scope of al-Sahili's actual contribution, he was traditionally linked with expanding Musa's court in Niani and building several mosques, including the famous and still standing Djinguereber Mosque in Timbuktu. Regardless of his actual architectural achievements, al-Sahili certainly helped transfer some knowledge and cultural influences from the Arab world, which was undoubtedly helped by numerous other less famous visitors.

While the architectural expansion under Musa was notable and well-remembered, his mark on Malian society went beyond that. He helped develop the Sankoré Mosque in Timbuktu into a fully-fledged madrasa (an Islamic school or university). It became a center of education, with a library that supposedly had the largest book collection in Africa since the Library of Alexandria. Other madrasas were set up in cities like Djenné and Ségou. The influx of various Arab scholars and teachers, along with a number of mosques being built across the empire, helped to further the Islamization of the empire, which was supported by Musa. However, he never forced the religion on his subjects. Another consequence of the spread of Islam was the gradual penetration of Islamic law into Mali's court and life, though it didn't completely replace the traditional rules set up by Sundiata. All of these civilizational trends gained traction after Mansa Musa returned from his hajj in late 1325 or early 1326.

The growing Islamization of the Mali Empire, regardless of its cultural enrichment of the Malinke civilization, proved to be the most long-lasting and important aspect of Musa's reign. While Islam had already been present in the region, it was only during Musa's rule that Islam began to truly take over as the dominant religion. This created a new cultural layer that could act as a social adhesive and connect different tribes and ethnolinguistic groups in West Africa. Thus, Islam became the cohesive force for the Mali Empire. It was something that Mansa Musa seems to have been aware of since he used his hajj to promote his prestige on a local level, as many previously turbulent regions grew to accept his reign. Such an approach seems to have been most notable in the eastern regions of the Mali Empire, around Timbuktu and Gao. As for longevity, Musa's other achievements are mostly gone now, even most of his architectural projects. Yet today, Mali and other regions that were once part of his empire are roughly 95 percent Muslim. Of course, the spread of Islam can't be solely attributed to Mansa Musa, but his contribution can be ranked as one of the most significant factors.

However, the Islamization of Mali proved to be a double-edged sword. While it was mostly peaceful and compatible with the native traditions, there were some differences that couldn't be easily erased. These proved to be less troublesome than in the case of the royal family. According to Sundiata's traditional law, the succession was officially patrilineal, but there was an addendum of sorts. It stated that power shouldn't be relinquished to a son while one of his father's brothers was still alive. In contrast, Islamic law firmly advocated the succession of the eldest son. Additionally, relying on Islam also required a ruling emperor to achieve a certain level of religious prestige to garnish the support of non-Malinke tribes and nations. Both of these factors would prove to be important once Mali began reaching its peak, and they would play a role in its downfall.

A depiction of Musa holding a golden coin in a late 14th-century European atlas.

The first glimpses of that came when Mansa Musa died, either in 1332 or more likely in 1337, after spending twenty-five years on the throne. As he wished, he was initially succeeded by his son, who became Mansa Maghan. His rule was rather short, as he died in 1341. Musa's brother Suleyman succeeded him, following the more traditional line of inheritance. Some more recent scholarly research tried to tie this to the spread of the 14th-century bubonic plague, more famously known as the Black Death. However, the evidence is sparse and inconclusive. The more likely scenario is that Maghan was deposed by his uncle, who took the throne for himself. Despite that, it seems Mansa Suleyman was a fitting heir for the great Musa, as he proved able to keep the empire relatively stable and prosperous during his nearly twenty-year-long rule.

The few details that were left about Suleyman's rule give us glimpses of how difficult that task was. For example, around 1352/3, he thwarted a coup that had been organized by his primary wife and a member of the Keita dynasty. However, some modern scholars claim he fabricated these accusations as political machinations of the court. Apart from that, Suleyman was often depicted as frugal or greedy, giving fewer gifts and taking more taxes than his brother. While he might have been more inclined to gather riches than Musa, it seems more likely that Suleyman was simply more fiscally responsible. He was possibly trying to recover the imperial treasury after his brother's expenses. Another possibility is that if the plague really reached Mali, the lack of labor caused an economic depression, forcing him to act and spend more soundly. It is also suggested that, for the same reason, he strengthened diplomatic and merchant ties with the Maghreb states since Egypt itself went through a plague-induced crisis. There are some indications that a few of the towns may have rebelled during his reign, while the border regions became targets of foreign raids, all of which added more hardship for Suleyman.

Even so, the Arab sources still reported on the splendor of the Malian court and cities, giving the overall impression that the golden age of Mali was still ongoing during his reign, even if it was in a slight decline. However, it all hinged around having a capable and strong mansa on the throne, one who could preserve what generations of Keitas had built. Unfortunately, with the death of Mansa Suleyman in 1360, the Mali Empire lost that kind of stability, signaling the actual start of its decline.

Chapter 5 – From Grandeur to Desolation

Through hard work, the Keita dynasty created a great empire that spanned from the Atlantic Ocean to the heart of the Sahara. It had millions of people, vast fertile fields, and gold, copper, and salt deposits. Once it achieved its peak, it seemed as if it was never going to fall. Yet, it turned out that it was built on faulty foundations.

The crumbling of the Mali Empire began immediately after Suleyman's death, as another succession civil war broke out. The opponents were Suleyman's son Qasa (Kassa) and Maghan's son Mari Djata (Konkodugu Kamissa in oral tradition), who possibly stood at the center of the failed coup of 1352. Initially, Qasa was crowned, but his reign lasted only nine months. He was most likely killed by his cousin, who became known as Mansa Mari Djata II. Unlike previous clashes over imperial inheritance, this seems to have grown into a full-out civil war. It was remembered as a bloody struggle, with much wider divisions within the empire. As such, it eroded the central government's power, especially since the two Keita camps were preoccupied with their internal struggle. However, there are no details on how the civil war affected Mali's periphery, but it is suggested that around that time, part of the Senegambian coast, which would eventually become the Jolof (Wolof) Empire, broke off from Mali.

By late 1360, the ordeal had ended, and Mari Djata II was the emperor. Had he been a competent ruler, Mali's decline might have slowed or even reversed, as was the case in some previous upheavals. Yet, according to Arab sources, he was a tyrannical and careless ruler, undermining everything his predecessors had worked on. Mari Djata managed to empty the royal treasury with his reckless choices, and corruption and cruelty became synonymous with his reign. The entire governmental system was on the brink of collapse. Total dissolution was only avoided because he contracted a sleeping illness, dying in 1374.

His son took over the throne, becoming Mansa Musa II. He reportedly tried to revert the actions of his father. Though he was remembered as a just emperor, he lacked the strength to repair the damage that had been done. Even worse, his imperial authority had been usurped by his chief advisor, who was supposedly named Mari Djata as well. According to Arab sources, Musa II became more of a prisoner and a puppet for his advisor or minister, prompting the question of whether his ascension to the throne was planned from the beginning.

During Musa II's rule, the Keita court continued to lose its power and stature, leading to the restless eastern provinces rising up in open rebellion. In response, Mari Djata charged the imperial forces to quell these revolts in order to stabilize the crumbling empire. However, it seems the easternmost provinces, most likely around Tadmakka, some 310 miles (500 kilometers) northeast of Timbuktu, managed to liberate themselves from the imperial rule. Nevertheless, Mari Djata was successful in keeping most of the empire together. Yet, the frequent uprisings, civil wars, and the general lack of safety and certainty began to slow down trade, which gradually deprived Mali of its primary source of revenue and strength. Overall, while the minister usurped imperial authority, he proved to be at least somewhat capable of keeping the empire afloat.

Thus, the situation worsened in 1387 when Mansa Musa II died, which caused Mari Djata to fall as well. His successor was Musa's brother, who became known as Mansa Maghan II. His reign was brief, and sources leave no details on it. However, since his rule was cut short by a coup in 1389, which was led by his high councilor, it can be assumed he was a weak ruler, most likely another puppet.

The usurper became known as Mansa Sandaki, though Sandaki was not his name but rather the title of the high councilor. Since he held the same position as the previous usurper Mari Djata before becoming the emperor, some historians speculate the two of them might be the same person. However, there is no clear evidence to support that claim. If that was the case, it would be likely that the Arab sources would mention it. In any case, Sandaki tried to gain some legitimacy by marrying Musa II's mother. Despite that, his rule was short and unsuccessful, unlike the previous usurpers. He was deposed and killed in 1390 by a member of the original branch of the Keita dynasty, reportedly the grandson of Mansa Qu, which would mean he was related to Mansa Yérélinkon and Sundiata. After seizing the throne, he became Mansa Maghan III, though some Arab sources mention him as Mahmud as well. While it seems Maghan III finally managed to shrug off the usurpation of imperial authority from within the court, he wasn't capable enough to keep the Mali Empire safe from foreign forces.

The Tuareg tribes from the Tadmakka region began to raid the Malian domain in the Middle Niger, most notably targeting Timbuktu. Similarly, the Mossi tribes from present-day Burkina Faso raided the area around Djenné. The populations of the targeted regions began to express their dissatisfaction with Mali's sovereigns, as they weren't able to protect them. This created a new wave of secessionism in the eastern provinces. Mansa Maghan III died between 1400 and 1404, yet there is somewhat of a gap in rulers in the sources. The next emperor mentioned was Mansa Musa III around the 1440s, but it is not clear if he was a direct successor of Maghan III or if there were one or more mansas in between them. The latter seems more likely, especially since the Mali Empire continued its decline, something that would most likely be reversed if someone ruled for forty years.

In the early decades of the 15th century, the eastern provinces fell one by one, most likely to the Tuaregs. The most impactful was the final loss of Timbuktu in 1434. Around the same time, other important cities, like Gao, were either conquered by the Tuaregs or proclaimed independence. Among the latter was Djenné, which briefly formed its own kingdom.

All of that amounted to the total loss of the Sahel territories of the Middle Niger River. The control of the trade routes passed into the hands of the new rising power in the area, first the Tuaregs, followed by the Songhai, who would create a new empire. Despite that, the Mali Empire still had firm control over its provinces in the savannah, as well as some on the Atlantic coast. According to some traditions, Musa III even managed to expand Malinke rule over part of the Wassoulou region, which was southeast of Manding and located in present-day Ivory Coast. Regardless, it was clear that the Keita dynasty's power was dwindling. In the mid-15th century, Musa III died, most likely around 1460, and he was succeeded by his younger brother, who is traditionally known as Gbèré. He became known as Mansa Uli II, the same Arab name given to Sundiata's heir. However, the exact succession line, relation between Uli and Musa, and dating are based on a few unreliable sources, leaving a lot of room for error.

Regardless of the rulers' names, reigns, and order of inheritance, it seems that the Keita dynasty remained firmly in control of Mali. Yet, the second half of the 15th century brought even more pressure on the empire. In the west, in the 1460s, the Songhai Empire sprang up from Gao, taking control of the Sahel from the Tuaregs. It also captured Méma (1465), one of the oldest provinces under Malinke rule, as well as Timbuktu (1468) and Djenné (1473). By the late 15th century, Songhai stood firmly in control of the trans-Saharan trade, though the trade was primarily based on salt and slaves. The Mossi also returned, and in the 1470s, they conquered Wagadou, the core of what was once the Ghana Empire, though that region was soon taken by the expanding Songhai Empire. All the while, Songhai pressured Mali from the northeast. On top of all this, the Portuguese arrived on the Malian coast during the 1450s, and they initially raided Mali's coastal provinces.

However, the Portuguese quickly realized that they would achieve much more by trading than attacking. Thus, by the 1460s, the Europeans abandoned their aggressive approach in favor of diplomacy. This created a new trade route and a source of income for the Mali Empire, which probably softened the blow of losing its dominion over the land routes. The arrival of the Portuguese also brought additional information about the coastal region, something that was much less interesting to the Arab writers. What they reported showed that despite all the setbacks, Mali still had some authority left. While the Jolof state in modern-day Senegal was, by then, a long-lost province, the region of Gambia was still firmly under Malian rule. More than that, the Europeans saw the Mali Empire as the most powerful state on the coast, and they also reported that the region was heavily populated by the Mandé people, implying a continuous migration and colonization from the hinterland.

The next attested change on the Keita throne came around 1481 when Mansa Mahmud II (Mamadou) became the ruler of Mali. Like his predecessors, he had little success in reverting the empire's decline. On the one hand, Songhai continued to expand, taking what was left of the northern provinces and spreading westward toward Jolof. Feeling the pressure of the new West African empire, Mahmud II welcomed the Portuguese embassies. He most likely hoped to expand maritime trade with the Europeans and possibly even attain some help in holding back the Songhai advance. However, the

Portuguese weren't interested in aiding any African state to become strong. Instead, these diplomatic missions to Mali, as well as to other nations in the region, were aimed more at gathering information about the nation's strengths, weaknesses, and opportunities. Furthermore, they gave better trade deals to smaller coastal chiefs, which was a calculated move. The goal was to strengthen them at the expense of their imperial rulers. The same Portuguese plan enfolded in their Gambian possessions.

Unfortunately for the Mali Empire, Mahmud II wasn't aware of that. Thus, while the Portuguese eroded his control over the coast, he asked them for an alliance to fight against another threat. This threat was the Fula people, who either conquered or liberated themselves from Malian rule in the Jalo region, located in the Fouta Djallon. While they began cutting off the Keitas from the coast, the Portuguese decided to stay out of the fight. Then, around 1496, Mansa Mahmud II died and was succeeded by Mansa Mahmud III. He inherited a weakened state, which was slowly crumbling from the foreign pressures on almost all its borders. It can only be presumed that Mali's inner politics and stability were far from ideal. For that reason, it may be unjust to mark Mahmud III as the worst or least capable ruler of the Mali Empire. Yet, at the same time, it was under his reign that Mali lost most of its territories. It reverted back to being little more than one of the local kingdoms.

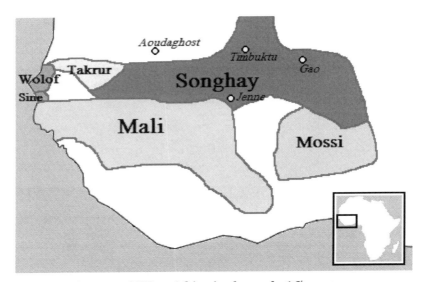

A map of West Africa in the early 16th century.
(Credit: Gabagool, CC BY 3.0 <https://creativecommons.org/licenses/by/3.0>, via Wikimedia Commons; https://commons.wikimedia.org/wiki/File:WestAfrica1530.png)

The first major troubles began in the early years of the 16th century, as the Songhai Empire, under the reign of Askia the Great, once again attacked Mali. After defeating one of Mahmud's generals, Askia took control of the Diafunu province, which was located north of Manding. With that loss, Mali lost all its territories north of its core. Soon afterward, the Fula managed to create their own empire based in present-day northern Senegal. Known widely as the Empire of Great Fulo, this state began pressuring Mali and gradually took over its northwestern provinces.

All the while, the Mali Empire was losing revenue, reputation, and military might, growing weaker with every loss. Like his predecessor, Mahmud III turned to Mali's only possible ally: the Portuguese. Around 1534, he tried to negotiate an alliance with one of their missions, but the Europeans were more interested in scheming and trade than in wars and expenses. The next harsh blow came in 1537 when the province of Kaabu managed to throw off the Malinke rule. Even worse, the newly formed state was also keen on taking more land from Mali, and it conquered Mali's western coastal provinces.

That cut off Mali from its only major trading point and also added a new threat to its borders.

The worst blow for Mali and Mansa Mahmud III came in 1545 when the Songhai Empire attacked once again. Not only did the Songhai beat the Malian forces, but they also invaded Manding itself. In the process, they sacked and occupied Niani, Mahmud's capital and the traditional center of Keita power. Mali's emperor was forced to flee for the first time since Sundiata had founded it. Mahmud reportedly hid in the mountains and forests of Manding, gathering what was left of his loyal troops. By early 1546, he had managed to gather enough forces to repel the invaders and prevent the complete subjugation of the Malinke. After that, he abandoned Niani as his capital, transferring his court to Ka-Ba. By the end of Mahmud's rule in 1559, Mali was more or less left with only the Manding region, its core province. By then, the Keita dynasty was left with only the memory of their former power and glory, most likely preserving their local rule based on the achievements of their previous rulers.

Nevertheless, the empire survived for a few more decades. However, there are no historical sources on the events or the rulers of the latter half of the 16th century. This is a clear indication that Mali had lost all of its importance and was an empire in name alone. Some historians even suggest that there was no mansa, though this seems unlikely. A more plausible theory is that there was internal strife for the throne, possibly a series of short and inconsequential reigns. In any event, around 1590, a new emperor emerged. Mansa Mahmud IV briefly showed some sign of Mali's and the Keitas' previous fervor and capabilities. He sought to exploit the downfall of the Songhai Empire, which had been brought on by internal crises and the Moroccan invasion. Mahmud IV's true desire was to return Mali to its former glory. First, he secured the alliance of some minor chiefdoms and regions that were once ruled by his predecessors, including some of the Fula tribes. Then he gathered his own troops, and in 1599, he marched to attack Djenné, which was still an important trading hub.

The Malian forces were substantial, and they proved to be a fierce opponent to the Moroccan forces. They attempted to charge the city twice but were repelled by the defenders. There were three prominent reasons for Mali's loss. First off, the Arab forces had gunpowder weapons, including cannons. Yet, this wasn't crucial, as even under heavy fire, the Malian army didn't scatter but fought valiantly, even though they wielded almost the same weapons as Sundiata or Musa I. The second reason was that the Fula allies betrayed Mahmud. Not only did they stay out of the battle, but they also gave the Malian plans to the Moroccans. Finally, Mansa Mahmud IV wasn't able to levy all of the Manding forces, as sources mention he was not accompanied by his most capable commanders. It shows that despite the façade, even Mali within the Manding region was fractured. Regardless, victory was within Mali's grasp, as the Arabs barely edged them out. The courage and capability that Mansa Mahmud IV showed were enough that even the Moroccan allies showed respect to him after the battle. It was the final dying breath of the Mali Empire.

After the loss, Mahmud returned to Manding, most likely abandoning any further ambitions. The respect he had gained for himself and Mali, as well as the rising new powers north of Manding, is what most likely prevented Mali from facing any substantial consequences of its loss. Thus, Mahmud reigned peacefully, at least in terms of foreign disturbances, until 1610. According to oral tradition, after his death, even Manding lost its unity. His three sons divided the lands, effectively ending the Mali Empire, even though they still called themselves mansas. The last known member of the Keita dynasty, Mama Maghan, was recorded as a ruler in one of the Manding chiefdoms around 1670. Yet, by then, the trans-Saharan trade was dying, as it suffered from constant wars and clashes in the Sahel, as well as the rise of maritime trade. With that, the region was left divided into small and relatively insignificant kingdoms and chiefdoms, with minor local powers attempting to dominate the region. Yet, none ever reached the heights that had been achieved by the Mali Empire.

Chapter 6 –The Malinke Civilization

While the previous chapters gave a somewhat detailed overlook of how the Mali Empire traversed the historical tides, there are only scattered depictions of its social and cultural life. Yet, without at least some basic introduction, the story of Mali wouldn't be complete.

The first important notion to be remembered is that the Mali Empire, pretty much from Sundiata's reign onward, was a multicultural and multinational state. It covered vast territories and oversaw many different people groups and tribes. These can be broadly separated into three groups—the Saharan nomads, the Sahelian peoples, and the tribes of the savannah and the coast. Examples of the nomads are the Tuaregs, the Messufa, and the Godala, among others. All of these belonged to the greater ethnolinguistic group of the Berbers. In the Sahel, there were the Songhai, the Soninké, and the Toucouleur, which were the most prominent ones. All of them belonged to different ethnolinguistic families. Finally, the most diverse was the southern Malian regions. There were the Jolof, the Fula, the Biafada, the Balante, and the Felupe. Then there were several Mandé groups, like the Bambara, the Soninké, the Soso, and many other smaller tribes. Of course, the last and the most important group was the Malinke. Although the various Mandé tribes shared some similarities, the entire Mali Empire was a rather diverse state. This is important to keep in mind.

To fully comprehend the disparateness, it is important to note that at Mali's peak, its population was estimated to be about forty to fifty million people. It covered some 480,000 square miles (roughly 1,240,000 square kilometers). With that in mind, it is clear that covering all these groups would be a tremendous task, more akin to covering all of West Africa rather than simply Mali. Thus, the main focus of this chapter will be the Malinke, with some societal aspects and details that may also be linked with other Mandé peoples or even other people groups.

However, before diving into the culture of the Malinke, there is another significant fact to be pointed out regarding the size and diversity of the Mali Empire. For most of this book, it was implied that the Keita rule spread over other regions or tribes, but for simplicity, the nature of the exact form of rule wasn't discussed. For that reason, it may seem that, at least in the political sense, the empire was a homogenous unit.

Yet, that is far from the truth. In reality, the direct rule of the mansas was most likely limited to Manding and possibly some closer regions like Soso, as the *Epic of Sundiata* implies. Other regions and provinces merely accepted the sovereignty of Mali through what could be roughly described as a system between vassalage and a confederation. It is difficult to pinpoint its exact nature since it is likely that the relationship between local and central authorities varied across provinces and time. However, it is clear that regional chiefs and kings paid tribute, while the mansa provided security and acted as the highest level of judicial authority. Nevertheless, in most cases, the Keita emperors didn't deal with local matters and issues, which were under the jurisdiction of the tribal chiefs. Despite the loose structure of the Mali Empire, the court remained the undeniable center of power and wealth.

At the very epicenter of power and the imperial court was, of course, the mansa. There is no need to further define his authority and roles. Nothing limited the emperor's power, at least in theory; as seen in previous chapters, they could become puppets. However, it should be mentioned that through his judiciary role, he became a "father of his people," the patriarch of all of his subjects. Even the commoners had the right to complain to him about their chiefs, governors, or whoever was representing the local authority in a certain region. At that highest legal level, the traditional law was commonly practiced. In contrast, the Islamic laws were more common on the local level, represented by judges often appointed by the emperor or his court.

Traditionally, mansas were surrounded by imperial councilors and advisors from noble clans. Their authority and roles changed according to the empire's capabilities and strength. There were also several more distinct offices. The most distinguished was probably the imperial griot. His job was to act as "the voice" of the mansa, most notably through the coordination of couriers, heralds, and criers, who came and went from the capital, spreading orders and returning with information. Griots were experienced in constitutional procedures, and they also acted as a master of ceremonies and the tutor of princes. According to the *Epic of Sundiata*, he was also tasked with keeping the emperor "grounded," which means he probably acted as a notable counselor. In the beginning, the position was hereditary, and it was passed on through the clan of Sundiata's griot. While there is no clear indication if that law was followed in the later stages of the empire, it was a distinction that made griots closer to mansas than other officials. They also initially played a religious role, acting as court magicians.

There were other central government offices, but the sources and traditions give us very little information on them. There was a general who most likely acted as the commander-in-chief or highest military advisor. There was also a master of the treasury who dealt with financial matters like gathering revenues and taxes and possibly overseeing imperial granaries. Other offices may have been similar to the later Songhai administrative structure, which seems to have been inspired by the Malian government. Thus, it is likely mansas also had councilors or ministers for foreign or diplomatic relations, as well as an inspector general for internal matters. It is also possible the court had masters of waters and forests, who were most likely tasked with exploiting and preserving those important resources. However, scholars cannot be sure about how those offices functioned, what their exact jurisdictions and tasks were, or if one person could have held more than one position.

Another layer of the central government was the Gbara or the "Great Assembly." This assembly met once a year, and it played an advisory role since it allowed the clans to voice their thoughts and issues with the mansa. However, since the members were mostly from the original Manding clans, they represented, for the most part, the Malinke population of the Manding region. That is why the Gbara was closer to the central government than many other assemblies. What is important to point out is that craft guilds also had representatives, as Sundiata assigned those to particular clans. This means that guilds had official political power, which wasn't a common notion in national assemblies.

Looking beyond the Manding, there were other provinces, including the vassals, of the Mali Empire. According to some sources, there were twelve provinces at the height of the empire. However, this number is dubious at best. There were likely more than just twelve provinces, as the same number is connected with the lands and tribes Sundiata allied with and conquered to form the empire. Thus, while it is possible that the later mansas tried to keep the number at the traditional twelve provinces, it is more likely that there were more, especially if vassal lands were included.

Regardless, we will move away from our discussion of the central government and talk about the provincial governors (*farbas*) and vassal chiefs or kings. The emperor placed the *farbas* to control important regions more directly, such as trading centers. Another possibility is that the governor was placed in newly conquered areas or ones prone to rebellion. *Farbas* were usually either members of the Keitas or a trustworthy Manding noble clan.

However, once the local population's loyalty was secured, control was reverted to an indigenous chief, who was given the title of *dyamani-tigui* ("province-master"), regardless of their traditional local title. Thus, they became more akin to vassals than provincial governors, though there are some indications of supervision through an imperial representative, usually a *farba*. Under normal circumstances, most of the *dyamani-tigui* were chosen by traditional methods or inheritance rules, but they needed to be confirmed by the mansa. Of course, those lands that peacefully accepted Malian sovereignty were only required to show their respect through tributes, with their ruler remaining in control. Additional assurance of loyalty seems to have been hostages of local chiefs. Below the provincial government was the *kafo-tigui* ("county-master"), who was usually appointed by the province-master. The village community itself commonly picked the *dougou-tigui* or "village-master."

Apart from governmental offices, there were also prestigious military titles. In the early days of the empire, these were less important and diverse, as most of the military command was still directly performed by the mansa. The only notable ranks were the *ton-tigui* ("quiver-master"), leaders of the sixteen noble warrior clans who acted as commanders of elite cavalry forces. Apart from that, there was the far less dignified position of *kèlè-koun* ("war-head"), commanders of regular infantry forces who usually came from the minor nobility. However, in later periods, especially after the great expansions of the 14th century, the military structure became more layered. Beneath the emperor, who still acted as the commander-in-chief, there were two primary generals whose theoretical authority was geographically divided. One was known as *farima-soura*, whose job was to protect the northern borders and traders, while *sankar-zouma* had the same task on the southern borders. These titles were most likely derived from the names of the regions in which the commanders were stationed. While their primary roles became a mix of civilian and military administrative offices, it seems they were also given other missions than just fending off raiders and bandits. Thus, they probably also led armies in offensive and defensive wars, acting like trusted and capable generals.

Below the two generals were the *farariya* or "brave," commanders whose position came from the *ton-tigui*. These were distinct nobles who led armies with their officers and were most likely part of the court and the government. Nevertheless, the *ton-tigui* remained a separate title, and it was given to *farariya* who served in the Gbara. The *farima* ("brave man") was a slightly less prestigious rank, whose role is sometimes compared to a European knight. A *farima* was also a member of a noble clan, but he commanded only a single cavalry unit, similar to the original *ton-tigui*. However, he also had a *kèlè-koun* report to him directly, allowing for combined actions of infantry and cavalry. In some cases, the *farariya* or *farima* could also become the *farba* of a province they conquered, but their holding of a civilian title was usually brief. However, the *farba* also had a military role, regardless of whether the position was filled by a Malian knight. His job in overseeing a province also meant he could assist local chiefs with defense in extraordinary circumstances. In that case, the *farba* commanded the cavalry, while the *dougou-kounnasi* ("impressive man at the head of the land") commanded an infantry force. Another distinction from the regular army was that these garrison troops were mostly slaves.

All of these officers commanded an army that reportedly had 100,000 men, out of whom 10,000 were a part of the cavalry elite. Yet, these numbers almost certainly varied across time and according to need. The core of the army was usually the Malinke soldiers from the Manding regions, and they were accompanied by their closest allies. The mansa could call up reinforcements from other provinces as he saw fit. Most of the warriors were freemen, who usually brought their own weapons. These were often regarded as heirlooms. The infantry was usually divided into the bowmen, who used poisons to compensate for their lack of penetrative power, and the spearmen, who also carried reed shields. Sabers and swords were usually only carried by the *kèlè-koun* or other higher officers. Another common weapon was the javelin, which was usually thrown at the start of a battle. As for armor, if they wore any, it was made from leather. The noble cavalry also used bows and spears or sabers, and only the richest could afford imported iron helmets and chainmail armor.

Slave soldiers or *sofa* initially only acted as squires for the nobles, but over time, they grew into a separate unit of warriors whose equipment was supplied by the state. What is interesting is that these slaves were able to advance through the ranks, even reaching the title of *farba*. This was because they were seen as more loyal since their entire fortune rested on their relations with the mansa, who was their master. Because of that, as well as Sundiata's law regarding the treatment of slaves, slavery in Mali seems quite different than other places around the world. Male slaves, traditionally known as *jonow*, were initially tasked with serving the nobles and transporting their goods, while females or, as the Arabs called them, *jawārī*, were given domestic tasks. Their role in agriculture seems to have been limited, as working in a field was seen as a mark of a freeman.

However, as the empire expanded and the people's needs grew, they were placed in various mines, mostly copper and salt, which made their labor more arduous. Additionally, the female slaves were also used for sexual exploitation by their masters. The slaves were seen as a trade commodity, and they were first sold to the Arabs and then to the Portuguese. Human trafficking increased later on when the Mali Empire began losing other resources. According to some sources, merchants could have had anywhere between one hundred and two hundred slaves each, and they were used to carry goods between the Sahel and the Sahara. Similarly, it has been said that

Mansa Musa had some twelve thousand slaves with him on his hajj. Thus, it could be said that slavery was common in Mali. Despite some leniency and the possibility of government offices, slavery in the Keita empire shouldn't be romanticized or downplayed in its cruelty. Like anywhere else in the world, most slaves' lives were far from good, and they depended on the benevolence of their masters more than any laws.

Nevertheless, it is an overstatement to say that the slave workforce was the main source of labor or trade; in other words, slaves were not a primary driving force of Mali's economy. That distinction belonged to agriculture. The majority of freemen were farmers whose occupation was praised in traditional songs. The respect heralded by agricultural jobs was such that even nobles occasionally participated, while the slaves usually didn't partake in them. Overall, both the Arab and the Portuguese sources mention that Mali had an abundance of food and that it was common for farmers to offer parts of their harvest to the mansa or the government. The crops also varied, as did the climate in the empire. Rice was grown near great rivers, such as the Niger and Sankarani, as well as in wetter regions like Kaabu and Senegambia. Beans, yams, and other various vegetables were grown in slightly less moist regions, while the drier climate in the Sahel was more suitable for millet, which required less water and irrigation.

The Sahel was also the primary animal-rearing region, even though it was spread across almost the entire empire. The livestock varied between cattle, sheep, and goats. An additional source of meat came from hunting, which was yet another praised vocation. It was also practiced by the nobles, who had no fear of losing their status. Quite the contrary, achieving the status of master hunter was one of the highest dignities among the Malinke. Hunting, which was done mainly with bows, also provided valuable hides for trade. However, it seems it was practiced more as an additional and supplementary activity rather than a primary occupation. Contrary to that, fishing was a very specialized profession, and it was present on almost every large river as well as the coast. To ease transportation and trade, fish was often smoked or dried, making it available across the empire.

Besides agriculture, another important economic branch was crafts. While there were many various trades, several were glorified to the degree of having their representatives in the Gbara. Probably the most notable was ironworking, as the blacksmiths were often depicted in oral traditions as mages and wise men. In the *Epic of Sundiata*, it was a blacksmith who helped young Sundiata overcome his disability and gain supernatural strength. In reality, their importance was derived from the fact that they produced various farming tools and implements, as well as much-needed weapons. The magical aspect of their craft was most likely a residual belief carried from the days of early metalworking. An additional sign of the significance of ironworking was the fact that there were great imperial forges in Niani. The development of that craft was helped by the fact that the Manding mountains were rich in iron, which made the rarer copper more valuable. It should be noted that it was a common practice for blacksmiths' wives to be potterers, and they probably utilized the same furnaces for their products.

In addition to blacksmiths, there were other notable crafts present in the assembly. There were the jewelers and goldsmiths who turned raw gold into much-coveted signs of wealth and social status. Leatherworkers were also important, as they created sought-after items, from shoes to leather armor and helmets, as well as cushions and other decorations. These items were also status symbols. Less influential but also important were the weavers' materials. They created colorful clothing, as well as various decorations such as rugs. These were made from cotton, which was produced within the empire. The items made by all of these artisans were important trading goods. All of the crafts, at least initially, were divided between the clans, and their products and rights were protected by laws and tradition. This was likely because they played such a vital role in the economic, military, and everyday life of the Mali Empire.

With that in mind, it is somewhat surprising that the merchants didn't receive this special protection or political representation, especially since they were sources of prosperity for the empire. It is possible this was because a number of traders were foreigners, as well as the fact that with enough wealth and political influence, they could threaten the nobility and even the imperial dynasty. Regardless, while the basis of Mali's economy lay in agriculture, the motor driving the empire was trade, both local and international. The most valuable goods were gold, copper, salt, kola nuts, cotton, and slaves. These were transported either on foot by using slaves and animals such as donkeys or camels or were carried on boats along the larger rivers. The most commonly used routes also had staging posts on them, while long-distance trade was usually conducted indirectly with one or more middlemen.

It is important to note that for a long time, trading was primarily done through the trans-Saharan trade network, as the Atlantic trade began later and blossomed only after the fall of the Mali Empire. Apart from that, Malian traders also dealt with the peoples in the south and southeast, with kola nuts being the primary resources they imported. However, having developed gold production within its borders allowed Mali to rise higher than any other West African empire before or after it. In fact, it is likely that the Malian goldmines were the largest producers of gold in the "Old World" at their height; they were only surpassed after the exploration of the Americas. Yet, despite the incredible amount of gold, it seems that Mali never developed a currency. Instead, they used the barter system as the basis of trade. Gold dust and nuggets were used as a common bartering item, though their value varied across different regions.

A 19ᵗʰ-century carving depicting traditional griots.
(https://commons.wikimedia.org/wiki/File:GriotsSambala.jpg)

While the traders weren't represented in the Gbara, the griots had two seats. The term "griot" itself is of European origin. In the Manding languages, the proper expression is *jeli, jeliw, djeliw,* or some other similar variation of the word meaning "blood." As it was seen with the imperial griot, it was a highly praised vocation. However, griots weren't tied only with the Keitas. Every noble family had to have a griot of their own, and it was common for almost all the villages and towns to have at least one. One of their primary roles was to remember and recite past events through traditional songs and keep records of the past. Since there weren't any written chronicles or documents, that role made them crucial for the functioning of the empire. Similarly, to this day, they represent one of the crucial historical sources of the Mali Empire, as oral traditions are still being passed on by new generations of *jeli.* Nevertheless, it should be noted that literacy existed, as reported by the Arab sources. The Arabic script was used but almost exclusively for diplomatic correspondence and possibly for mundane needs, not for record-keeping.

Because of the griots' vast memory and knowledge, they were often asked for advice and to act as arbitrators. Since being a griot required years of training and since their indispensable role required loyalty and trustworthiness, they were treated like other notable crafts. For these reasons, their trade was to be kept within two clans, as ordered by Sundiata. However, seeing griots as merely record-keepers is denying them their artistic and cultural roles. Their songs were accompanied by music, which they played. They played various traditional lute-like instruments like the kora, the khalam, the balafon (a large wooden xylophone), or even some types of drums. Griots told stories about great feats, as well as more mundane things. While many tales and songs were passed on through them, they also composed new ones if there was a need for them. With all that in mind, they could be seen as central figures in maintaining the cultural identity not only in Mali but in most West African societies, as their presence wasn't limited only to the Mandé people.

Apart from griots, who represented both literature and music, the Malian society also had other arts. Firstly, it should be pointed out that the griots weren't the only musicians; there were also performers whose role was closer to simple entertainers. They played various types of drums, trumpets, and stringed instruments. From depictions of the royal palaces, it is clear that their walls were painted, reportedly with vibrant colors. However, the exact content and details of all this are unknown, but they were most likely highly inspired by Islamic art. Yet, it seems paintings weren't a prominent part of the Malian culture. Various sculptures and carvings were more common and celebrated. The pottery figurines seem to have been the most predominant. These depicted realistic portrayals of humans, usually warriors either on horses or with bows, but there were also depictions of ordinary people and other animals. Everyday pottery and textiles were also decorated, usually with geometric patterns. In the case of pottery, it was done by carving or painting, while with the textiles, this was achieved either during the weaving or dyeing processes.

On a larger scale, the Mali Empire also had its own architectural style. It is part of the wider Sudanian-Sahelian architecture design, which is characterized by building with adobe and plaster. The buildings have large wooden beams that stick out of the walls and other surfaces. Its structure was dictated by local needs. The lack of stone made adobe a primary building material, while wooden beams were needed to give additional structural support to the mudbricks. Additionally, these logs stuck out of the walls for decoration but acted more as scaffolding since the intense heat caused the walls to melt, requiring frequent repairs. In general, the Sudano-Sahelian style predates Mali, but during its time, the style was used in grander projects.

On the outside, the Malian-styled buildings usually had a mud-colored façade, and it was mostly undecorated. Apart from the beams, it was only adorned by small cones or pinnacles, but in some cases, they used towers. These details were at least partially inspired by the Arab building style, which Mansa Musa tried to replicate. Today, the most well-known example of this style is the Great Mosque of Djenné, which was originally built around 1330, if not earlier. Afterward, the Malian substyle influenced others in the region. However, in most cases, this grand building style was used for building mosques, palaces, and other great projects. Common homes and buildings were much simpler.

The Great Mosque of Djenné today, a great representation of classical Malian architecture.

Overall, the culture of the Mali Empire shows a clear mixture of traditional and Islamic influences and ideals, creating a unique civilization. On the outside, especially from the modern perspective, it looks more Islamic and has strong Arab influences. This was due to the Keita mansas deciding to pursue Islamization. Yet, medieval Mali was far from being a completely Islamic state. While the imperial family, along with many nobles and merchants, converted, Islamization wasn't forced, and there was a strong traditional community. In fact, the frictions between the two groups caused many frictions within the empire. Thus, it can be concluded that Muslims weren't a clear majority. It is even possible, especially in the early periods of the empire, that Muslims were a minority. With that in mind, traditional West African religions should be touched upon, as Islam is a better-known faith.

However, giving a simple description of the traditional belief system is hard since it had local variations, and in some regions, these traditional religions have been completely erased. Yet, some basic notions can be recreated. In most cases, nature, spirits, and ancestors were worshiped, possibly to the level of deities. They usually had some kind of shamanic priest who held knowledge and helped with religious interpretations. Ceremonies were also present, and they sometimes revolved around communal singing and dancing, among other things. It is possible they practiced some kind of fortune-telling and sacrifice, though not of humans. They definitely practiced fetishism and the veneration of relics. While relics created connections with the past and their ancestors, fetishes were seen as magical objects that could bring good fortune, strength, and power. Some of these ideas were mixed with Islam, like, for example, great respect for the jinn, which resided in nature, or holding onto the idea of talismans and charms.

What the two religions had in common was that they allowed for polygamy, where a single man could have more than one wife. Furthermore, while according to Sundiata's traditional law, women were to be respected and treated properly, it seems that in most cases, they were unequal to men. Sundiata's rules were dictated as if told to other men, treating women like objects of the law. Furthermore, there is no evidence they had any specific rights, except for divorce in case a husband couldn't provide for his wife, suffered impotence, or had some kind of madness. While some queens and imperial concubines are mentioned by name as important persons, it seems that, in general, women played mostly secondary roles. They were linked with domestic duties and responsibilities.

Today, there is a prominent practice of female genital mutilation in West Africa, and it is possible this practice existed at the time of the Mali Empire. However, there is no clear evidence for this claim, as it isn't mentioned in any source. Regardless, it is clear that Malian society was male-dominated, like most other civilizations of that time.

Even so, the civilization of the Malinke, and thus the rest of the empire, had its own unique traits. It was formed over a long period of time, mixing various influences and responding to changes that occurred within and around it. Yet, its importance is much wider than the Mali Empire itself, as it also influenced many other cultures and civilizations. Some of its aspects are still present in modern-day Mali and West Africa.

Conclusion

The tale of the Mali Empire is one filled with struggles, great rulers and puppets, distant journeys, trading, expansion, wars and conquests, and losses and disasters. Within all of that, the story of Mali is of a unique civilization and a great realm. Yet, at the same time, it shares some commonalities with so many other empires and kingdoms throughout history and the globe. It had laws and politics, diplomacy with distant lands, and enemies and allies. However, more importantly, its story fills the gap in African history, which, in the past, was often disregarded as less important. Not only that, but it also shows that Mali and the rest of Africa weren't irrelevant or separate from the world in pre-colonial times.

The wealth of Mali, as exhibited by Mansa Musa's extravagancies, echoed across the Mediterranean world, capturing the imagination of his contemporaries. The Mali Empire was constantly trading and exchanging ideas and knowledge, and it sought to establish its presence in the world. It certainly succeeded there, as the memory of its greatness is preserved through oral traditions and the culture of modern West Africa. Hopefully, with this guide, its history has reached a wider audience, filling in the blank places on the canvas of history. We should also be reminded that Africa has many more stories like this that deserve our attention if we want to have a better grasp of our present world.

In a somewhat contradictory manner, the tale of the Mali Empire also showcases that history itself has a lot of gaps to be filled. There are many uncertainties that have to be filled with guesses and estimations. However, those blank pages can only be filled with the hard work of new generations of historians and archaeologists, as well as new research and projects. In the end, the history of the Mali Empire, as well as history in general, is constantly reminding us that humans have always been interconnected.

Here's another book by Captivating History that you might like

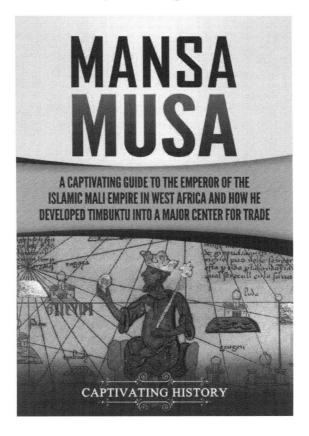

Free Bonus from Captivating History
(Available for a Limited time)

Hi History Lovers!

Now you have a chance to join our exclusive history list so you can get your first history ebook for free as well as discounts and a potential to get more history books for free! Simply visit the link below to join.

Captivatinghistory.com/ebook

Also, make sure to follow us on Facebook, Twitter and Youtube by searching for Captivating History.

Bibliography

A.G. Hopkins, *An Economic History of West Africa*, Routledge 2020.

Barker, Graeme; Goucher, Candice (2015). *The Cambridge World History // The Tichitt Tradition in the West African Sahel*, 499–513.

Basil Davidson, *The Growth of African Civilisation: A History of West Africa 1000–1800*, Longman 1985.

D. T. Niane, *General History of Africa IV - Africa from the Twelfth to the Sixteenth Century*, U N E S C O Publishing 2000.

D. T. Niane, *Sundiata - An Epic of Old Mali*, Pearson Longman 2006.

David C. Conrad, *Empires of Medieval West Africa: Ghana, Mali, and Songhay*, Chelsea House 2010.

David C. Conrad, *A Town Called Dakajalan: The Sunjata Tradition and the Question of Ancient Mali's Capital*, The Journal of African History, 35 (1994), pp 355-377.

Emmanuel Akyeampong, *Themes in West Africa's History*, Ohio University Press 2006.

François- Xavier Fauvelle, *The Golden Rhinoceros - Histories of the African Middle Ages*, Princeton University Press 2018.

G. Innes and B. Sidibe, *Gambian Version of the Mandé Epic*, Penguin Classics 1999.

J. D. Fage and R. Oliver, *The Cambridge History of Africa Volume 2: From c. 500 BC to AD 1050*, Cambridge University Press 2008.

J. D. Fage and R. Oliver, *The Cambridge History of Africa Volume 3: From c. 1050 to c. 1600*, Cambridge University Press 2007.

John K. Thornton, *Warfare in Atlantic Africa 1500–1800*, UCL Press 1999.

John O. Hunwick, *Timbuktu and the Songhay Empire: Al-Sa'di's Ta'rikh al-Sudan down to 1613, and Other Contemporary Documents*, Brill 2003.

Levtzion N. and Spaulding J., *Medieval West Africa: Views from Arab Scholars and Merchants*, Markus Wiener Publishers 2003.

Levtzion N., *The Thirteenth- and Fourteenth-Century Kings of Mali*, The Journal of African History, 4 (1963), pp 341-353.

Levtzion Nehemia, *Ancient Ghana and Mali*, Methuen 1973.

M. de Villier and S. Hirtle, *Timbuktu – The Sahara's Fabled City of Gold*, Walker Publishing 2007.

Michael A. Gomez, *African Dominion: A New History of Empire in Early and Medieval West Africa*, Princeton University Press 2018.

Nawal M. Bell, *The Age of Mansa Musa of Mali: Problems in Succession and Chronology*, The International Journal of African Historical Studies, Vol. 5, No. 2 (1972), pp. 221-234.

Ousmane O. Kane, *Beyond Timbuktu: An Intellectual History of Muslim West Africa*, Harvard University Press 2016.

P. J. Imperato and G. H. Imperato, *Historical Dictionary of Mali*, Scarecrow Press 2008.

R. Oliver and A. Atmore, *Medieval Africa 1250–1800*, Cambridge University Press 2004.

Robert S. Smith, *Warfare and Diplomacy in Pre-colonial West Africa*, Methuen & Co 1976.

Made in the USA
Monee, IL
23 August 2022